FOR LOVE, SEX, AND DATING

Relationship Goals

LIFEWAY
GIRLS
DEVOTIONS

publishing team

Director, Student Ministry
Ben Trueblood

Manager, Student Ministry Publishing
John Paul Basham

Editorial Team Leader
Karen Daniel

Content Editor
Stephanie Cross

Production Editor
Brooke Hill

Graphic Designer
Kaitlin Redmond

Published by LifeWay Press®

No part of this work may be reproduced or transmitted in any form or by any means, electronic or mechanical, including photocopying and recording, or by any information storage or retrieval system, except as may be expressly permitted in writing by the publisher. Requests for permission should be addressed in writing to LifeWay Press®, One LifeWay Plaza, Nashville, TN 37234.

ISBN 978-1-0877-4262-5
Item 005831571
Dewey Decimal Classification Number: 242
Subject Heading: DEVOTIONAL LITERATURE / BIBLE STUDY AND TEACHING / GOD

Printed in the United States of America

Student Ministry Publishing
LifeWay Resources
One LifeWay Plaza
Nashville, Tennessee 37234

We believe that the Bible has God for its author; salvation for its end; and truth, without any mixture of error, for its matter and that all Scripture is totally true and trustworthy. To review LifeWay's doctrinal guideline, please visit www.lifeway.com/doctrinalguideline.

Unless otherwise noted, all Scripture quotations are taken from the Christian Standard Bible®, Copyright © 2017 by Holman Bible Publishers. Used by permission. Christian Standard Bible® and CSB® are federally registered trademarks of Holman Bible Publishers.

table of contents

04 intro

05 getting started

06 God's design for sex

26 God's design for marriage and gender

40 what is outside of God's design?

60 how do we love people who don't follow God's design?

72 articles and resources

intro

From day one, little girls are presented with the idea of prince charming and a future husband who will sweep her off of her feet. And we always remember our first crush—you know, the cute guy you notice sitting across the classroom, and the very mention of his name makes you blush?

You begin to obsess over whether or not he thinks you're cute. You check social media every five seconds to see if he's liked one of your posts, commented, or sent you a message. You may shyly send one of your friends to ask him if he likes you back, or maybe you boldly walk over and ask him yourself. You might have even felt the heart-racing, jittery, giddy feelings a crush brings.

The Greek word associated with this feeling is eros—romantic love. This love is different from friendship, parental, or even unconditional love. This love is the connection you feel for a guy that causes you to risk your heart on the chance that he might feel the same way as you do.

What might begin as butterflies in your stomach eventually turns into deep feelings, governed by desires that are hardwired into you. The truth is that God designed you to feel deeply and with a longing to be loved. While we may talk about relationship goals in the sense of those picture-perfect couples or representations of what we want in our own dating relationships, God has different relationship goals for us than what we see in the world. God has a specific design for the way His people love one another—even in romance.

But He doesn't leave us on our own to handle all the feels we have when it comes to our crushes or boyfriend; instead, He gives us the answers we need in His Word. And His Word speaks transparently and with certainty about the right way to engage in love, sex, and dating.

It's so important for us to understand God's design for love, sex, and dating—and there's no better way to understand than to explore what God's Word says. So, open your Bible, your heart, and your mind to what God has to say, and be ready to embrace the life long journey of eros love—living out God's relationship goals for you by enjoying His design for love, sex, and relationships.

getting started

This devotional contains 30 days of content, broken down into sections that answer a specific question about love, sex, and dating. Each day is divided into three elements—discover, delight, and display—to help you answer core questions related to Scripture.

discover

This section helps you examine the passage in light of who God is and determine what it says about your identity in relationship to Him. Included here is the daily Scripture reading, focus passage, along with illustrations and commentary to guide you as you study.

delight

In this section, you'll be challenged by questions and activities that help you see how God is alive and active in every detail of His Word and your life.

display

Here's where you take action. Display calls you to apply what you've learned through each day's study.

prayer

Each day also includes a prayer activity in one of the three main sections.

Throughout the devotional, you'll also find extra articles and activities to help you connect with the topic personally, such as Scripture memory verses, additional resources, and quotes from leading Christian voices.

Section 1: GOD'S DESIGN FOR SEX

day 1

THAT'S IN THE BIBLE?!

discover

READ SONG OF SONGS 4.

You have captured my heart, my sister, my bride. You have captured my heart with one glance of your eyes, with one jewel of your necklace. How delightful your caresses are, my sister, my bride. Your caresses are much better than wine, and the fragrance of your perfume than any balsam. — Song of Songs 4:9-10

Have you ever sat by a bonfire, mesmerized by the dancing flames? Fire is mesmerizing and useful for warmth, cooking, and creating necessary items for everyday life. However, fire can quickly rage out of control, so it must be handled carefully. Fire is a good thing; it's one of God's greatest gifts to us. However, if not treated with care and respect, it can be deadly.

What does fire have to do with Song of Songs? Well, in this book of the Bible, we see God's clearest instruction on romantic love. Here, we find a clear description of God's design for love, sex, and relationships. The message is beautifully displayed in poetic form—a mixture of figurative and literal language—and covers many of our big questions about God's design for sex.

Today's Scripture reveals what many girls desire when we think of romantic relationships: a husband gushing over his new bride. He wasn't shy about expressing how she made him feel. The rest of the book goes into great detail about the beauty of sex and God's design for it. It's not a dirty or gross thing. It's like fire—a good, helpful, necessary gift from God that demands our respect and care.

LifeWay Girls | Devotions

delight |

Unfortunately, our world has taken God's good gift and let it spiral out of control, like wildfire burning through a community. Destructive attitudes and practices about love and sex have become popular ideas in our culture. This doesn't diminish God's design, but it calls for His people to understand His desires and diligently obey Him.

How would you describe your attitude toward sex up to this point in life?

List some ways your views were similar to and/or different from the ones shared in Song of Songs 4.

display |

One of the greatest ways we can display God's love for humanity is by modeling His design for love, sex, and relationships. While we might find ourselves at odds with our culture by practicing a Biblical worldview, we can do this in a loving and thoughtful way. How we believe is as important as what we believe.

What attitudes do your friends have about love, sex, and dating?

People will always talk about love, sex, and dating, so it's important to know God's design. Dig into Song of Solomon, check out commentaries, talk with a trusted adult like your parents or youth pastor, and then write out God's design in your own words. This will help you be prepared to have tough conversations.

> **Ask God to give you an open heart and mind, as well as a willingness to submit to His lordship in your life—even over love, sex, and relationships.**

Relationship Goals

day 2

PERFECT MATCH

discover

READ GENESIS 2:18-24.

And the man said: This one, at last, is bone of my bone and flesh of my flesh; this one will be called "woman," for she was taken from man. This is why a man leaves his father and mother and bonds with his wife, and they become one flesh.
— *Genesis 2:23-24*

There are a lot of famous duos: like peanut butter and jelly; tacos and Tuesday; Anna and Elsa. They are good alone, but together they are amazing! Some things are just better when paired with their perfect match.

Today, we look back to the beginning—when God created humanity. The first human he created was Adam. God gave him a place to live and almost everything he would need. Adam was alone, so God offered him all the animals He had created, but there wasn't a true companion for Adam. Then God made Eve. When Adam first saw her, he knew he had finally found his perfect match.

God blessed the match and instructed them. This man and woman were perfectly matched. God's design for marriage and sex—from the beginning—is and has been for one man to unite his life in marriage with one woman. They will spend the rest of their days together in a loving relationship, separated only by death.

delight |

Matthew Henry wrote, "The woman [Eve] was ... not made out of his [Adam's] head to rule over him, nor out of his feet to be trampled upon by him, but out of his side to be equal with him, under his arm to be protected, and near his heart to be beloved."[1] God created man and woman equally; perfectly complementary to each other in every way.

How have you seen the Biblical teaching on marriage of one man, one woman, for one lifetime lived out?

In what ways has today's devotion challenged your perspective on God's design for dating, marriage, and sex?

> One way God displayed His perfect love for us is through His provision for companionship. Thank God for His perfect provision and love!

display |

Whether you get married one day or not, ask God to begin working in your heart now to help you treasure His design and desire for love, sex, and dating. On a blank sheet of paper, draw a circle and write the word *treasure* in the center. Outside of the circle, write anything that comes to mind when you think about being treasured.

Treasuring God's design—for yourself as a girl made in His image, as well as those of the opposite gender—means recognizing that God made men and women to be equal. Ask the Holy Spirit to guide you as you examine your heart. Ask yourself: *When am I tempted to treat guys as if they're not my equal? When do I feel like I'm less than as a girl?*

We honor God when we treat people with love and respect. On an index card, write out *I will love and respect all people* as a reminder of God's design for humanity.

Relationship Goals

day 3

A GOOD GIFT

discover

READ GENESIS 1:26-31.

God blessed them, and God said to them, "Be fruitful, multiply, fill the earth, and subdue it. Rule the fish of the sea, the birds of the sky, and every creature that crawls on the earth." — Genesis 1:28

Sex is a good gift from God. The Bible makes it clear: sin distorted and perverted God's good gift. The moments of today's passage took place in a perfect world before sin. Adam and Eve were a perfect match, in a perfect place, with all they could ever need. Then, He gave Adam and Eve not only the ability to create more life, but the command to create more life. If sex within God's design as outline in the Bible was dirty, gross, or wrong, then our holy God wouldn't have commanded us to participate in it.

After the different things God created throughout the first five days, God looked at what He had done and He saw it was "good" (Gen. 1:4,10,12,18,21,25). But on the sixth day of creation, only after He created humanity and told them to "be fruitful" and "multiply," did He proclaim that it was "very good" (Gen. 1:31). When we approach sex with care and respect, participating in it God's way (within a biblical marriage), it is a very good thing.

This passage reveals one of the purposes of sex: procreation. If not for sex, there would have been no way for Adam and Eve to populate the earth and obey God's command to be fruitful and multiply. It's important to note that this doesn't mean everyone will get married or have kids, just that this is one part of God's beautiful design for His people.

delight |

God doesn't tempt us or lead us to sin (Jas. 1:13). So, God's command to Adam and Eve would not have led them in a way contrary to His will. God gave them to each other to be committed in a marriage relationship for their whole lives, creating a family that honors Him.

When we talk about sex as God designed—and not in crude or flippant ways—we can show respect for sex. How do you talk about sex with others?

Do you think the way you talk about sex honors God's design? Why or why not?

> **If you have not cared for your life in a way that honors God, don't be discouraged! You still have infinite worth and value. Confess to God where you've fallen short of caring for your life and His creation. Then, ask Him to help you take better care of things in the future.**

display |

On a scale of 1 to 10, with one being "Not at All" and 10 being "Completely," rate how well you feel like you care for the people and things God has placed in your life.

List two changes you can make this month to honor God through the way you care for all of creation—including His people.

Relationship Goals

day 4

BY DESIGN

discover

READ PROVERBS 5:15-23.

Let your fountain be blessed, and take pleasure in the wife of your youth. A loving deer, a graceful doe—let her breasts always satisfy you; be lost in her love forever. — Proverbs 5:18-19

Imagine this: You've bought the cutest sweater, but you want to wash it before you wear it. It's so easy to wash a sweater the wrong way, only to have it draw up or become a mess of fluffs and pills. If you read the care tag on the inside of the sweater, you'll likely be able to wear it (and love it!) for a long time to come. But if you wash it the wrong way, you may not even get to wear it once.

The Book of Proverbs is built around wisdom, much of it told from the perspective of a father to his son. While the perspective is from a masculine point of view, the wisdom here applies to either gender: It's OK—in fact, it's right— for married couples to enjoy sex. But, like washing your sweater, it's very important to go about it the right way.

God created sex to be pleasurable, and it is—inside and outside of marriage. The truth is when we experience sex the way that God designed, the pleasure is even greater! Walking in God's intended design for every part of life brings us greater joy. Living life God's way leaves us fulfilled, blessed, and grateful.

delight

It's important to acknowledge and appreciate that God created sex for pleasure, too! He wants us to enjoy His good gift; He just wants us to enjoy it His way. What are other examples of things that are best when done the right way?

God's design of sex for pleasure reveals His character. He gives us good gifts, but He also gives us rules to govern His gifts. His instructions are for our good. How does it affect you to know that the boundaries God placed around sex are for our good? How will it help you set good boundaries in dating relationships?

display

Ask the Holy Spirit to guide you as you examine your heart. Do you feel like any of God's commands aren't for your good? Why?

Go back and read Proverbs 5:22-23. How could following God's design for love, sex, and dating bring life? Why would doing the opposite bring destruction?

> Consider any areas of your life where you fight against God's instruction and confess them to Him. Ask God to help you understand His design and purpose. Seek to submit yourself to His desires for you and trust that His love for you is greater than your love—even for yourself.

Relationship Goals

day 5

FAITHFUL

discover

READ EXODUS 20:1-17.

"Do not commit adultery." — Exodus 20:14

Imagine a volleyball game. Visualize the players skillfully dashing around the court passing, setting, receiving, and spiking the ball. Now, imagine the referees just walk out. Suddenly, the players start diving under the net, running out of bounds to receive the ball, serving only four feet away from the net, or even beginning with an attack rather than a serve. These things are against the rules in volleyball. But if they weren't, there would be no way to actually play the game—it would be complete chaos!

Just like the rules of the game tell us how to play volleyball, the Ten Commandments serve as rules that govern our lives. The first four commandments concern our relationship with God. The final six give instruction about our relationships with one another. Today, we're focusing on commandment number seven: "Do not commit adultery." While the technical definition of adultery concerns having sex with someone other than your spouse, Jesus also says that even looking at someone with lust means you've committed adultery in your heart (Matt. 5:27-28).

Marriage was designed for a man and a woman to be committed and faithful—sexually, emotionally, and mentally—to each other. This is a foundational rule that others build on. Complete faithfulness within marriage is necessary for trust and the health of the relationship. God's command concerning adultery helps us learn how to build strong, healthy, and God-honoring relationships and marriages.

> Maybe you've been affected by adultery. If so, talk to God about how it makes you feel. He is there for you. He understands and He cares. If you haven't been affected by adultery in any way, thank God for that, and pray for the married people you know to always remain faithful to one another.

delight |

Why is faithfulness so important in a relationship?

How can you grow in your faithfulness to God?

How can your relationship with God help you be faithful in your other relationships?

display |

God calls us to be faithful in our relationships because He is faithful to us.

Write out the word "Faithful." For each letter of the word, write a word or sentence that describes God's love and faithfulness toward us.

Young women of Jerusalem, I charge you by the gazelles and the wild does of the field,

do not stir up
or awaken love
until the
appropriate
time.

—SONG OF SONGS 2:7

day 6

THE RIGHT TIME

discover|

READ SONG OF SONGS 2:1-7.

Young women of Jerusalem, I charge you by the gazelles and the wild does of the field, do not stir up or awaken love until the appropriate time.
— Song of Songs 2:7

Think about your favorite song—whether you like to sing along, play the chords, or just listen. Maybe you've never thought about it much, but timing is vital in music. The entire band has to play at the right time for the song to work. If the drums begin early and the guitar plays late, then it would sound like pointless noise, not music. Keeping things in their time is important for both music and God's design for sex.

While the language in today's Scripture can make the meaning hard to decipher, this text portrays two people who have feelings for each other and want to be physically intimate. For example, the woman desired the embrace of the man she loved (v. 6). Instead of allowing her emotions to lead and her desire to have control, she reminded herself and the young women of Jerusalem that there is a time and a place for physical intimacy—and before marriage is not that time or place.

Song of Songs chapters three and four describe the marriage ceremony between the man and woman. Only after their wedding do they get the OK to begin their sexual relationship. Just like a band playing in time, sex has its time and place, too.

delight |

Unfortunately, our culture shares a completely different message about sex than this passage does. Why do you think God designed sex for marriage?

What issues could arise from having sex before marriage?

display |

Write out on an index card the words *I desire to be transformed each day to be like Jesus in the way I love others, date, and honor God's design for sex.* Use this card as a reminder to keep your focus on God, no matter what other relationships you have or don't have. If you're in a dating relationship right now, seek to honor God in that relationship.

Read Romans 12:1-2. Our culture can place a lot of pressure on people to conform, but God desires for us to conform to His way. List three steps you can take to renew your mind and conform to God's design when it comes to love, sex, and relationships.

> Sometimes people do "awaken love before its time." If this has been your experience, God's desire is not to shame you, but to give you grace when you repent and turn from your sin. Take a moment and pray a prayer of repentance and ask Him to help you remain committed to only having sex after you're married. If this has not been your experience, thank God for helping you not give into sexual temptation. Ask Him to help you remain faithful to His plan for sex.

Relationship Goals

day 7

EXTREME ACTION

discover

READ MATTHEW 5:27-30.

But I tell you, everyone who looks at a woman lustfully has already committed adultery with her in his heart. — Matthew 5:28

A popular church song for children warns, "Be careful little eyes, what you see."[2] What we look at is definitely important, and so is the way we look at it. It's possible to look at something that belongs to someone else and not sinfully desire it. However, when we look at something that is not ours and lust (intensely desire) to have it for ourselves, we cross the line.

This idea is what Jesus described in Matthew 5. He reminded His listeners that Moses taught them to not commit adultery (review day 5 for a refresher on this). Then, Jesus took it further: we have to do more than just not commit adultery; we must avoid committing adultery emotionally and mentally by refusing to look at someone else and lusting after them in our hearts.

Jesus gave an extreme solution to help us avoid this issue—if our eyes or hands cause us to sin, get rid of them (vv. 29-30). Let's be clear: Jesus didn't mean for us to take this teaching literally. Jesus wanted us to eliminate the opportunity to fall into sin. He wants us to take sin seriously and avoid it with extreme action.

LifeWay Girls | Devotions

delight |

Sometimes it's easy to look the part. Maybe it seems like we're avoiding sin, but our hearts are actively involved in it. What steps can you take to avoid sinful thoughts and attitudes and "purify your [heart]" (Jas. 4:8)?

How might your attitude need to shift for you to view your sin as seriously as God does?

display |

Do your devices lead you toward sin? Does social media? Do certain people? List some ways you can cut these things from your life so you can avoid temptation.

We are way more motivated to avoid sin when we focus on God's love for us rather than just keeping the rules. How can you turn your heart toward dwelling on God's love rather than just following His rules?

> Read 1 John 4:9-10. Focus right now on God's love for you. It's unending, immeasurable, and unmatched. Thank Him for that love. Then read 1 John 4:11, and ask Him to help you love Him in return.

Relationship Goals

day 8

NOT MY OWN

discover

READ 1 CORINTHIANS 6:9-20.

"Food is for the stomach and the stomach for food," and God will do away with both of them. However, the body is not for sexual immorality but for the Lord, and the Lord for the body." — 1 Corinthians 6:13

Have you ever let a friend borrow something that she didn't take care of? It's frustrating when she finally returns the item and it looks way worse than when you let her borrow it. When you let someone use something that's yours, you hope to get it back in the same—or better—condition. Like you entrusted your friend with your sweater or scrunchie, God has entrusted us with our bodies.

Paul had a lot to say about this in his first letter to the Corinthians. He explained that those who live in habitual unrighteousness will not inherit God's kingdom (vv. 9-10). If we have given our lives to Christ, then we have been washed by the Spirit (v. 11). This means we belong to Jesus, and our bodies are for His glory. We don't own ourselves anymore. So, our desires, wants, and even opinions must line up with His. He is our Lord.

Because He is our Lord and we don't own ourselves anymore (v. 20), we can't live for ourselves sexually or in any other way. We are called to take care of the body He has entrusted to us, and we do that by following His instructions concerning love, sex, and dating. Through the Holy Spirit, the Lord lives in us, guiding us, governing us, and helping us in every area of our lives. He is our Lord and has authority over us, so we must obey Him.

delight |

Our culture teaches that no one should tell us what to do with our own bodies. Christians believe that we are bought with a price and our bodies are for God's glory (v. 20). When we give our lives to Jesus in faith, our bodies are for His glory, plan, and purpose. Why might this be difficult for us to understand and accept?

What are some benefits of trusting God rather than our feelings?

> It's not easy to give control of our lives to God. Take a moment and ask Him for help in this area. He is trustworthy and has plans for your good.

display |

Jot down three ways you can display to the world that you belong to Christ.

God's love for us is unconditional and His plan is perfect. As you continually learn to give yourself to Him your faith, trust, and love for Him will grow. On a blank sheet of paper, take a minute to write out a poem or song of praise to God for His unconditional love and perfect plan.

Create a lock-screen with the words: I am not my own. Set it as both the background and the lock-screen on your phone for the rest of the month. When you see it, remember that Jesus is Lord of your life—not you.

day 9

LOVE AND RESPECT

discover

READ EPHESIANS 5:22-33.

To sum up, each one of you is to love his wife as himself, and the wife is to respect her husband. — Ephesians 5:33

Clownfish have a unique relationship with sea anemones. The anemones act as a home and protective barrier for the fish, while the fish give nutrients and protection to the anemones. This is called a symbiotic relationship, which forms when two organisms benefit each other and work together to live.[3] This relationship mirrors what Paul described in the passage for today.

Husbands and wives form a symbiotic relationship when they abide by what Scripture teaches. Husbands are to love their wives like Jesus loves the church, and wives are to respect their husbands. A wife needs her husband to love and cherish her, while a husband needs respect from his wife. God purposefully created marriage between "corresponding" people (Gen. 2:18).

However, the ultimate picture here is not of a marriage between a husband and a wife, but of Christ and the church. Jesus loves the church so much that He gave His life for her. As His bride, the church is to honor and respect Jesus. God created marriage to model how Jesus and the church function in a love relationship. As His people, we display this reality to a watching world, as Christian husbands and wives seek to love and honor each other in their marriages.

delight |

Marriage is intended to be a symbiotic relationship of mutual love and respect. How does this affect your view of the marriage relationship?

Marriage is designed to be a picture of Jesus and the church. In what ways does this truth enhance your view of marriage?

> **Unfortunately, many husbands and wives do not seek to love and respect each other. This might be the circumstance for your parents or other married people you know. If it is, pray for them right now. Ask God to help them grow in their relationship with Him and with each other. If the married people in your life do have a relationship where they seek to love and respect each other, thank God for that.**

display |

While you don't have a husband to love and respect at this point in your life, you can do these things for the Lord. List three ways you can show love and respect for God in your daily life.

Review the memory verse on pages 24-25 and seek to make it your desire to submit to Jesus' lordship in all areas of your life.

Relationship Goals

Section 2: GOD'S DESIGN FOR MARRIAGE AND GENDER

day 10

THE VOW

discover

READ MARK 10:1-12.

"Therefore what God has joined together, let no one separate." — Mark 10:9

God created marriage and gender—just like He created sex—with specific intentions. However, culture has altered God's plan, presenting other ideas as valid and even loving. But Scripture makes it clear that God's desire is not for marriages to end in divorce.

The Jewish Law permitted divorce, but as Jesus pointed out, this allowance was not from God. Rather, it was a result of hard hearts (v. 5). This means that divorce is an option in certain circumstances, but it's never the first path a married couple should take during difficult times.

At many marriage ceremonies, verse 9 is included as part of the vows. God designed marriage. When a Christian man and woman marry, they have (hopefully) sought God in faith and prayer, and He was the driving force that brought them together. Therefore, what God created—both the institution of marriage and the couple itself—no person should seek to break apart. This command to not destroy the union of the marriage applies to the couple inside the marriage as well as anyone outside of the marriage.

LifeWay Girls | Devotions

delight |

Jesus said that people's hardheartedness led to the allowance for divorce. What does it mean to be hardhearted?

How can we avoid becoming hardhearted toward God's desires for our lives?

> While you're probably years away from marriage, it's still important to have a soft heart toward God. Pray that God would soften your heart in places where you have allowed hardness to set in. Ask Him to open your heart to His desires for your life.

display |

Some critics of dating culture have called it practice for divorce because of how often young couples break up and get back together. If you're allowed to date, be cautious. Don't rush into it. Talk with God—and your parents—if you want to date.

If you are dating, model the respect and love that God teaches married couples to have. Consider that the person you're dating might not be the person you'll marry. Your boyfriend belongs to the Lord, not to you. Remember that as you set boundaries for your relationship physically, emotionally, and even in the ways you spend your time.

Ultimately, trust God with your future—even your relationship status. Read Jeremiah 29:11. Write this verse out on a sticky note and put it in a place where you'll see it.

day 11

PRITORIES

(PRIORITIES)

discover

READ 2 CORINTHIANS 6:14-18.

Do not be yoked together with those who do not believe. For what partnership is there between righteousness and lawlessness? Or what fellowship does light have with darkness? — 2 Corinthians 6:14

If you've ever participated in a three-legged race, then you know that the key to success is finding someone who's about as tall and strong as you. If your partner is considerably taller, shorter, weaker, or stronger than you, it's tough to match your stride. Then, you can't create a steady, unified motion with your legs tied together.

In today's Scripture, Paul expressed the same understanding about having mismatched spiritual relationships. The word picture he painted with the word "yoked" concerned animals. If you took a large and stronger animal and strapped it into a harness with a smaller and weaker animal, they wouldn't be able to work together. The stronger animal would overpower the weaker animal and drag it in the direction the stronger animal wanted to go.

As you grow and look for a person to unite your life with in marriage, it's important that you are not spiritually unequally yoked. If your relationship with God is the most important aspect of your life, the person you're dating needs to value his relationship with God just as much. If this element is out of balance, the more dominant person in the relationship will push things where they want it to go. Dragging someone along spiritually is difficult, and so is getting dragged away from God.

LifeWay Girls | Devotions

delight |

How have you seen this truth in your life or in the lives of girls you know?

What are some indicators that a person you're interested in—or dating—places the same importance on his relationship with God as you do? (Support your answer with Scripture where you can.)

> Ask God to help you seek out relationships with people who share your faith in God and will help you grow in Him and not be pulled away from Him.

display |

Believers need to have relationships with unbelievers to share the love of Christ with them, but the closest friendships we have need to be with other believers. Take an inventory of your relationships. Next to each title, write the names of a few people who fit the description.

Best friend(s):

Boyfriend/guy you'd like to date:

Friends:

Acquaintances:

Reflect on these questions as you consider your friendships. Are your closest friends believers who encourage you to be like Jesus? Are you heavily influenced by people who are not Christ followers? How can you best honor God in your friendships?

day 12

NOT FOR EVERYONE

discover

READ 1 CORINTHIANS 7:8,32-35.

I say to the unmarried and to widows: It is good for them if they remain as I am.
— *1 Corinthians 7:8*

If you type your friend's address into the GPS on your phone, you'll notice there are several ways to get there. One way might be the fastest, another might avoid highways, and another might avoid toll roads. Ultimately, every path leads to the same destination.

As Christ followers, the aim of our lives is to live for Him and bring Him glory. While Jesus is the only way to God, God has designed each of us with unique callings and ways to bring Him glory. God gave each of us different skills, interests, and passions. The way you serve God might not be the same as your parents or your best friend. Along those lines, it's also true that marriage is not necessarily the path for every person's life.

The apostle Paul was unmarried (v. 8). He went so far as to say that if someone is unmarried, it is good for her to remain that way. He explained that unmarried people have an ability to focus their lives on Christ that the married do not. Ultimately, it is not wrong for people to marry or remain unmarried. The aim of our lives should be to live as the Lord commands and obey His plan for us.

delight |

What advantage do single people have that married people don't when it comes to serving God?

How does it affect you to know that it's God's plan for some people to get married and some to remain single?

display |

Maybe you've dreamed of being a wife and a mom, and it scares or saddens you a bit to think that might not be God's plan for you. Take a minute to sit with those feelings. Journal a prayer to God, letting Him know exactly what's on your heart. Pray that you would willingly submit to whatever plan God has for your life.

Create a piece of art or print with the words of Romans 8:28. Place it somewhere you can see it often as a reminder that God can use all things—including marriage or singleness—for our good and His glory.

> **Do you know a single woman who is faithfully serving God and living for His glory? It's possible that she longs to be married. Pray for her to find fulfillment with whatever God plans for her life. If it's marriage, pray that God brings her spouse along soon. If it's to remain unmarried, ask God to help her be like Paul and take advantage of the opportunities she has to serve God with her life.**

Relationship Goals

day 13

UNIQUE AND INTENTIONAL

discover

READ GENESIS 1:26-27.

So God created man in his own image; he created him in the image of God; he created them male and female. — Genesis 1:27

A few years ago, there was a trend to reimagine a real historical figure or a famous book. In the new stories, the adversaries wouldn't be political opponents, Civil War, or romantic longing. No, the enemies would be...well, monsters. For example, movies were made with titles like *Abraham Lincoln Vampire Hunter* and *Pride and Prejudice and Zombies*. These alternate takes might be humorous, and they provide a totally different angle on the subject. However, it's not difficult to imagine President Lincoln or Jane Austen being appalled by the unique and creative direction given to their lives and stories.

When God created us, He made us male and female. From this Scripture, we clearly see that God had an intentional design for humanity, creating two distinct genders. While we refer to God in the masculine pronoun, both males and females are made in God's image. God created the genders to be unique from each other, and He was intentional in His design.

God does not intend for us, His creation, to mimic what Hollywood and literature have done. We are "remarkably and wondrously made" (Ps. 139:14). Our gender is not random, a mistake, optional, or fluid. Our gender doesn't require outside creative direction; rather our identity is intentionally and unmistakably given by the Creator of the universe.

delight |

You were created in the image of God. List any feelings you experience as you read this truth.

Because we are created in the image of God, we cannot be flippant or casual about the way He made us. How do you care for the body He has given you and treat it with the respect it deserves?

How can you encourage other girls to see and believe that they are remarkably and wondrously made and that God has a beautiful plan for their lives, which includes their gender identity?

display |

Read Psalm 139:13-16 and memorize verses 13-14. God knows you inside and out. He created you. You are remarkably and wonderfully made. You might not feel that way, but you are. You have value and worth simply because you are God's creation. You can't always trust your feelings, but you can trust the truth of who God is as revealed by His Word.

Finish this sentence: *I am made in God's image. I am remarkably and wondrously made because ...*

Name one thing that is wondrously unique about you that you love.

> There are no two ways about it—God loves you! Take a moment and meditate on that truth. If you have struggled to love yourself—or your birth gender—ask Him to let His love overwhelm you. Let His love open your heart.

Relationship Goals

day 14

LOVE > HATE

discover

READ DEUTERONOMY 22:5.

"A woman is not to wear male clothing, and a man is not to put on a woman's garment, for everyone who does these things is detestable to the LORD your God."

Today's Scripture speaks to a complicated topic in our culture today. The issue goes beyond wearing clothes of the opposite gender to understanding who God has made us to be. Gender confusion is a real thing that affects many people. This devotion is not meant to minimize it or belittle those who struggle with it. The goal is to help clarify what God's Word has to say about gender and how to understand it.

God's desire is for men and women to outwardly identify as men and women. The reality is that sometimes people are born different. In Matthew 19:12, Jesus spoke about eunuchs (men without distinguishing male anatomy). This passage acknowledged that a man might be physically different from other men, but Jesus didn't ever imply that they should identify as anything other than a man as a result of their physical differences.

These are challenging texts to weave together, but ultimately, God designed men and women the way He did on purpose (see day 13). When people try to change their gender identity, they operate outside of God's design. While this is clearly outside of God's desire and design, it doesn't give us license to express hate toward people who struggle with or even embrace gender confusion. God's love toward all people remains, and we—His people—are to follow His lead.

delight |

Why people suffer from gender confusion is a complicated issue. The bottom line is that the lordship of Christ is above our feelings, and even our biology. Genesis 3 explains that sin affects all of creation. It causes pain and difficulty where God did not intend pain to be found. He distinctly made two genders, yet as a result of our fallen world, confusion can arise from something quite simple.

People who suffer from gender confusion are made in the image of God. How can you be reminded that all people are made in God's image and therefore have infinite value and worth?

display |

You might have friends or know of people who suffer from gender confusion. Write three ways you can love them without compromising the truth of God's design.

Read Acts 17:16-34. Paul was distressed over the idolatry he found in Athens, but he did not attack them for it. Instead, he tried to find common ground so he could lovingly help them come to know Jesus. We should take the same approach when it comes to the issue of gender confusion.

> **Take a moment now and pray that God would help bring clarity from the confusion that sin brings to the world. Pray that you would always remember that love is greater than hate.**

day 15

UNIQUELY YOU

discover

READ LUKE 10:38-42.

While they were traveling, he entered a village, and a woman named Martha welcomed him into her home. She had a sister named Mary, who also sat at the Lord's feet and was listening to what he said. — Luke 10:38-39

If you have a brother or sister, it's likely she is quite different from you. Even if you do not have a sibling, you probably know siblings who are opposite from each other. They may share the same gene pool, but their differences are plain to see. This demonstrates how everyone is created uniquely—even people in the same family.

God made only two genders and created them with distinctions, but He did not create people within the genders to be exactly the same. Mary and Martha were quite different from each other. Martha was focused on work. Mary was focused on Jesus. Martha hosted. Mary listened.

In Jesus' day, women were typically supposed to do what Martha immediately set about doing—serve the men. Mary, though, took a seat at Jesus' feet like one of His disciples. While Martha was frustrated with Mary, Jesus pointed out that Mary had actually made the better choice (vv. 40,42). It's not wrong if your interests, abilities, and talents fall outside traditional gender stereotypes. Being locked into stereotypes is damaging and simply untrue. God made each person to have a unique set of interests, abilities, and personality traits.

delight |

List three things that you are interested in or skills you have. Praise God for the ways He has uniquely gifted you!

Martha wanted to be recognized for her efforts. Mary wanted to hear from Jesus. When have you been tempted to use your uniqueness for your own glory?

display |

Whether your interests get you labeled as a girly-girl or a tomboy, the important thing is that you use every gift and interest you have for God's glory. List three ideas for how you can glorify God with your interests, abilities, and passions.

God's desire is for us to be faithful to Him, not to a stereotypical version of your gender. Complete this sentence: *I will allow God to use me for His glory by …*

> **Thank God for making you unique. Ask Him to help you see yourself the way He does. Ask Him to help you use your gifts, passions, talents, interests, and personality for His glory.**

Relationship Goals

For it was you who created my inward parts; you knit me together in my mother's womb.
I will praise you because I have been remarkably and wondrously made.

Your works are wondrous, and I know this very well.

PSALM 119:13-14

day 16

ALL OF YOU

discover

READ 1 CORINTHIANS 6:12-20.

Flee sexual immorality! Every other sin a person commits is outside the body, but the person who is sexually immoral sins against his own body.
— *1 Corinthians 6:18*

Have you ever seen someone get so angry that she punched a wall? This might give a momentary release of anger or frustration, but the results are often more painful, like a broken hand. This is an instantaneous, gut reaction. Regardless, letting off a little steam in this way probably hurts the person more than whatever made her angry.

Most of the time we're pretty good at avoiding things that hurt us. But when something feels good, we often struggle to see how it might one day hurt us. This is the case when we engage in sexual activity outside of God's design. There's no getting around it; sex feels good. However, God's plan for sex—one man, one woman, one marriage, for one lifetime—is the best and only route that pleases Him.

Paul also made it clear that when we come to faith in Christ, we are now part of His body (v. 15). When we do something that hurts our body, we hurt His body as well. This is why Scripture tells us that our bodies belong to Jesus and we must glorify Him with how we care for and use our bodies.

> Ask God to help you be willing to give all of yourself to Him—not just your mind or the words you speak, but your entire body. Think of yourself as an instrument in His hands, and let Him use you for His purposes.

delight |

Along with abiding by God's plan for sex, how can you use your body for His glory?

Not everything is beneficial (v. 12). What are some of the negatives that come from not following God's plan for sex?

Scripture says sexual sin is a sin against the body, which is the temple of the Holy Spirit. How does this affect the way you view sexual activity that goes against God's design?

display |

Take God's word for it, and know that if you practice sex outside of God's design, it will hurt you eventually. Maybe you've already experienced this kind of pain. If so, journal a prayer to God, asking Him to heal you from the pain of your past and to help you glorify God with your body every day from now on. If not, journal a prayer to God asking Him to strengthen you to withstand sexual temptation and continue to honor Him with your body.

Read Matthew 6:33. Create a note on your phone that says: *I will choose God's kingdom and righteousness over my own desire.* Every time you see this note, commit to God that all that you are will be used for His glory. God will honor that and help you as you seek Him.

day 17

MY IDOL

discover

READ COLOSSIANS 3:1-11.

Therefore, put to death what belongs to your earthly nature: sexual immorality, impurity, lust, evil desire, and greed, which is idolatry. — Colossians 3:5

Imagine that you're sitting around with a few of your best friends, talking about the different singers, actresses, influencers, or maybe even speakers and writers you all love. Maybe someone even says something like: "She's awesome—definitely my idol!" In this case, an idol is someone you admire and respect an incredible amount. You might even want to be like her.

While it's OK—good even—to have godly women to look up to, the word *idol* doesn't always carry such a positive meaning. In a biblical sense, having an idol is a serious offense. In fact, it's such a serious offense that it's found in the Ten Commandments: "Do not make an idol for yourself" (Ex. 20:4). Scripture defines an idol as anything that you place before God.

All of the things Paul listed in verse 5 can be idols in our lives, including sex. It's dangerous and sinful to place anything above God in our lives because no one can love you perfectly like God can. God is all-knowing, and His very essence is nothing but pure love. When He says not to place anything above Him, it's not because He is a needy egomaniac; rather, this command exists because it's absolutely what's best for you.

LifeWay Girls | Devotions

delight |

In verse 9, Paul mentioned the old self and the new self. In the column labeled Old, list some characteristics of your old self. In the column labeled New, list some characteristics of your new self.

Old   New

> Take a moment and examine your heart. Scripture says we "once walked" in these old idolatrous ways (v. 7). Ask God to reveal how you may have slipped back into walking in these old ways of life. Ask Him to help you walk in the new way—His way—instead.

display |

Sex is definitely an idol for numerous people. It seems as if nothing is more important to our culture, whether it is their ability to love whomever they please or express their sexual identity however they want. With God's design in mind, what's the problem with this attitude about sexuality?

God designed sex and has a perfect plan for it in your life. List two steps you can take in your own heart to make sure that God is in His rightful place in your life.

day 18

IN POWER

discover

READ GENESIS 39:1-20.

Although she spoke to Joseph day after day, he refused to go to bed with her.
— Genesis 39:10

Maybe you know a girl who constantly stirs up drama in class, but never gets in trouble for it. Maybe she's such a good actor that people never suspect her, or maybe she's so charming she can talk herself out of trouble, or maybe she's even a teacher's kid. Regardless, when the class gets disciplined, this girl always seems to take advantage of her ability to get out of it.

It's wrong to use your abilities or the position you have to take advantage of others. But Potiphar's wife didn't live by those rules; instead, she tried to use her position of authority to take advantage of Joseph sexually. She tried and tried to seduce Joseph—who was a slave in her household—but he held strong to his conviction in the Lord and his loyalty to Potiphar. Despite the fact that Joseph continually did the right thing, he was eventually framed for an offense he didn't commit and sent to prison.

While Joseph's story eventually had a happy ending, this Scripture shows him in a bit of a rough patch. A woman was seeking to use her power over him to get what she wanted—and even though he did what was right, Joseph was punished for it. Simply put, regardless of your position or power, it's never right to take advantage of someone else.

LifeWay Girls | Devotions

delight |

Joseph called it "immense evil" for him to sleep with Potiphar's wife (v. 9). Why would sleeping with another man's wife be evil? Explain.

When have you done the right thing but still gotten in trouble or accused of doing something wrong?

When you do the right thing and still face negative consequences, how can you remain faithful to God—like Joseph did—and continue doing the right things?

display |

Think about the abilities and positions of authority you have in your life. List two ways you can use these things for good and not evil; to help serve others rather than take advantage of others.

> In recent years, there have been countless reports of people in positions of power using their authority to take advantage of others sexually. It's possible that you have been sexually abused by someone in power. If this is the case, report this to the proper authorities and get help. Take a moment right now and pray that the Lord would give you courage to take this step. If you have not been abused by someone else, pray for those who have and be an ally for them. Use the resource provided to help them get the help they need.

Relationship Goals

day 19

CLOSE TO THE EDGE

discover

READ 1 THESSALONIANS 4:1-8.

For this is God's will, your sanctification: that you keep away from sexual immorality, that each of you knows how to control his own body in holiness and honor, not with lustful passions, like the Gentiles, who don't know God.
— *1 Thessalonians 4:3-5*

Did you know that you can ride a mule to the bottom of the Grand Canyon? With a team, you'll follow a very narrow trail to the Colorado River, which runs through the base of the canyon. It's a 10.5 mile trip down and it takes about 5.5 hours.[4] Mules aren't exactly known for their intelligence. In fact, they are prone to walk as close to the edge of the canyon as possible. This trip is not for the faint of heart.

Sometimes people treat sex the same way. In an attempt to seek a thrill, they try to get as close as possible to the edge of what's right without falling over. It's a dangerous place to be because it's tough to turn back from the draw of sex. The promise of pleasure often clouds our judgment. In today's Scripture, Paul warned the Thessalonians to avoid all forms of sexual immorality. That is not limited to sexual intercourse, but includes oral sex, intimate touching, pornography, and any activity that causes you to lust.

People often want to know: "How do I know where to draw the line?" This is a reasonable question, and the answer is to do what honors the Lord and the other person. Does this activity lead to holiness and deepen your relationship with God, or is it selfish? Things that push you away from God should be avoided at all costs.

Pray that God would help you to honor Him with your body and mind in your relationships. Don't try to get as close to the edge as you can. The edge is closer than you think.

delight |

How can you honor God by practicing self-control with your mind and body?

Why does it dishonor you and others when you cross the line sexually?

display |

Sanctification is the process of growing in holiness (v. 3). List three ways you can grow in holiness when it comes to your relationships with guys.

Scripture teaches plainly that the instruction to not get close to the edge when it comes to sex is not just there to take away your fun. The instruction is God's desire and is ultimately what's best for you. Name one way you can actively accept God's instruction in your life and not reject His desires for how you use your mind and body sexually.

Relationship Goals

day 20

UNFAMILIAR

discover

READ 1 JOHN 2:15-17.

For everything in the world—the lust of the flesh, the lust of the eyes, and the pride in one's possessions—is not from the Father, but is from the world.
— *1 John 2:16*

When someone moves from one part of the country to another, she often speaks with an unfamiliar accent. When she speaks in her new town, you might hear people ask her, "You aren't from around here, are you?" It can be easy to identify where a girl is from by how she speaks, but it's more difficult to identify what a girl stands for just by the sound of her words. Just like people who have an unfamiliar accent may seem strange to you, Christians will seem strange to the rest of the world because of the way God has called us to live.

John reminded Christians that lust is not of God, but from the world. Lust is when you look at something that is not yours and have an unholy desire for it. It's the exact temptation that draws people to pornography. Pornography has become acceptable in our society. It's easy to access on the internet, and it's almost assumed that people engage with it regularly. Pornography is not from the Father; it's destructive to both the viewer and the people making it. It demeans and devalues people and expresses the wonderful gift of sex in a way that does not honor God. Our voices must stand unified on the destructive nature of pornography. We must be identified as people from the Father who speak with love, who cherish people and don't devalue them, and who avoid the lust of the flesh and eyes.

LifeWay Girls | Devotions

delight |

Review Matthew 5:28 and compare it with 1 John 2:16.

Read 1 Corinthians 6:19-20. How does avoiding pornography glorify God with your body?

When we follow after the Father, people often look at us and think, "They aren't from around here." This is a compliment. It means we aren't living like everyone else and are pursuing holiness. Jot down two ideas to help you stand apart from the world when it comes to pornography.

display |

Unfortunately, it's likely you have been exposed to pornography at some point in your life. It's also possible that you struggle with an addiction to it. If this is the case, know that there is help for you. Memorize 1 Corinthians 10:13. Find an accountability partner who will walk with you through temptation. Use internet accountability software like Covenant Eyes®. Read and believe 2 Corinthians 12:10. Know that in your weakness, Christ is strong. Lean on Him.

Write the name of a girl you can approach to be your accountability partner.

> Read Psalm 51:10 as a prayer. Ask God to help you walk in purity and not be stained by worldly lusts.

day 21

IT'S OBVIOUS

discover

READ ROMANS 1:18-27.

Therefore God delivered them over in the desires of their hearts to sexual impurity, so that their bodies were degraded among themselves. They exchanged the truth of God for a lie, and worshiped and served what has been created instead of the Creator, who is praised forever. Amen. — Romans 1:24-25

Have you ever played a game where you look at two pictures that are basically the same, except for a few minor differences? Sometimes, when searching for those differences, you strain your eyes trying to find something small. Suddenly, you realize the thing you've been looking for is actually fairly obvious. Sometimes people are guilty of doing the same when it comes to God's design for sex.

In Romans 1, Paul explained what sin had done to numerous people in his day. He said that people suppressed the truth of the clear, evident existence of God (v. 18). They acted as if there was no God, so they exchanged what was true and good for what was untrue and not good (v. 24). The result was a sexual culture that denied what was obvious from God's design for humanity.

Paul made evident what he was referring to—both women and men gave into same-sex attraction. This is a very delicate subject in our world today, but the aim of this devotion is to help you understand what God's Word says about these serious topics. Romans 1 unmistakably reveals that God's design is not for people of the same gender to have sex with one another.

LifeWay Girls | Devotions

A big part of that reasoning is because it fails to fulfill part of God's purpose for sex—same sex genders can't biologically procreate. If same-sex attraction complied with God's design for sex, the ability to procreate would have been possible in same-sex couples, since His instruction from the beginning of time was to "be fruitful, multiply, fill the earth" (Gen. 1:28).

delight |

Aside from God's plan for sex, where do people most often fail to follow God's plan?

What other evidence of God's existence can we find in creation's design?

display |

While God desires for us to follow His plan in all things, He doesn't love us less when we fail. As His people, we must do the same. Unfortunately, countless people in our world do not follow God's design for sex. This doesn't mean you have permission to hate or belittle those people. On an index card, write the words: *I am called to love people even more deeply when they don't understand or live by God's design.* Tuck it in your Bible at today's Scripture. Every time you see it, remind yourself that you're called to love all people.

> **Pray for those who struggle with same-sex attraction. Ask God to help you love them, not in a condoning way, but in a gospel centered way.**

day 22

IS LOVE ALL YOU NEED?

discover

READ MARK 10:6-9.

"But from the beginning of creation God made them male and female. For this reason a man will leave his father and mother and the two will become one flesh. So they are no longer two, but one flesh. Therefore what God has joined together, let no one separate."

Many people feel the band The Beatles is the greatest of all time. Their catalogue of hits is so impressive that their cultural impact is still felt today, even though they broke up in the 1960s. One of their greatest hits of all time is a song called "All You Need is Love." These words have become a rallying cry today for many when it comes to marriage. But is love really all you need to have a happy, successful, God-honoring marriage?

Today's Scripture comes from a section of Jesus' teaching on divorce. Divorce was covered on days 10 and 11, but there is an important piece about God's design for marriage within this teaching. Jesus quoted Genesis 1:27 and 2:24, combining them to express God's ultimate design for marriage. Marriage is between one man and one woman, joining both of their lives and bodies together to create a new family that is not to be broken until death separates them.

Since this is God's design for marriage, there is no part of the plan that allows for people of the same gender to marry each other. This goes against those in our society who want to say love is all you need for a marriage. Obviously love—for God and for each other—is vital. But love is not enough if you want to follow Jesus'

LifeWay Girls | Devotions

teachings. Love must be coupled with God's design for a marriage to truly be God-honoring.

> Pray that as you grow, your desire would be to follow Jesus' teachings in every area, including marriage. Pray that your heart would be soft enough for Him to shape as He desires.

delight |

Why do you think it's best to follow Jesus' teachings on marriage and not just rely on loving each other for a God-honoring relationship?

How can you love people who don't comply with Jesus' teachings on marriage without condoning their disobedience to His instructions?

display |

You may know someone whose parents have a marriage that is outside of Jesus' teachings. Remember, she didn't choose her parents, and she should love, honor, respect, and obey them (Ex. 20:12). It's not your job to condemn her parents or shame her for their parents' decisions.

List three ways you can love and support people whose parents have not followed Jesus' teachings on marriage.

day 23

THE ELEPHANT IN THE ROOM

discover |

READ LEVITICUS 20:13 AND 2 CORINTHIANS 3:6.

He has made us competent to be ministers of a new covenant, not of the letter, but of the Spirit. For the letter kills, but the Spirit gives life.
— *2 Corinthians 3:6*

Have you ever heard the phrase, "We can't ignore the elephant in the room"? This means there is something big that no one wants to talk about, but needs to be addressed. When it comes to the biblical teaching on sex and same-sex attraction, the elephant in the room is Leviticus 20:13. How do we address this verse with those who don't agree with God's design for sexuality?

First of all, we shouldn't execute people for expressing same-sex attraction. In his letter to the Corinthians, Paul explained that we live under a new covenant. Under the old covenant, the Hebrews lived in a theocracy. This means that God was their king. Because God was their king, the Law found in the Old Testament was also the law of their land—their government and constitution.

Now that Jesus—God in flesh—has come, lived a perfect life, died on the cross, rose again from the dead, and ascended back to the right hand of the Father in heaven, the Old Covenant and all its regulations have been fulfilled. This does not mean we can ignore or pick and choose what we want to follow from the Old Testament. We still abide by the moral law taught in the first 39 books of the Bible. But we do not give the same legal consequences the Hebrews did because we do not live in a theocracy where God is the king of our government and His laws are the laws of our land. Therefore, we can eat shellfish, wear clothes made of two different materials (Lev. 11:10; 19:19), and we should not execute people who practice same sex attraction.

delight |

Keeping the Old Testament law never saved anyone. The point of it was to reveal our desperate need for a savior (Gal. 3:21-26). What led you to understand that you needed Jesus as your Savior?

> We all desperately need a Savior. Praise God for Jesus, who willingly gave His life so that you could have the chance to have a restored relationship with God, leading to eternal life.

display |

The spirit of the Old Testament and New Testament is the same: love the Lord your God and love your neighbor as yourself (Matt. 22:34-40). How can you love the Lord your God with all your heart, soul, and mind today?

Heart:

Soul:

Mind:

List two ways you can love your neighbor as yourself.

day 24

SPATIAL DISORIENTATION

discover

READ ROMANS 1:28-32.

And because they did not think it worthwhile to acknowledge God, God delivered them over to a corrupt mind so that they do what is not right.
— *Romans 1:28*

When a pilot flies through heavy clouds, spatial disorientation can occur. This is when a pilot can't see the horizon to know if the plane is level, turning, ascending, or descending. When the horizon is obscured, the pilot's senses can be affected, causing this feeling of disorientation. Between five and 10 percent of all aviation accidents happen because of spatial disorientation, and the majority are fatal.[5]

Humans need help knowing where the horizon is. We are sinful from birth, so our own senses are distorted by greed, lust, selfishness, and so on (Ps. 51:5). Paul explained that when people embrace these things that God clearly defines as evil, they experience moral spatial disorientation—they not only do these evil things, but applaud others who do them as well. Tragically, this is where our society is when it comes to sex. Many people don't know which way is up or down. Worst of all, they embrace destructive ideas that not only go against God's design for sex, but can cause painful consequences, all in the name of love.

God created sex, and He made the horizon. He determined what is up and down. He gave the instruction on what is best and what love really is. The further from Him we drift, the more dangerous our path becomes. Therefore, we must acknowledge Him and let Him determine our attitudes and actions concerning love, sex, and dating.

delight

How can we avoid moral spatial disorientation in our lives?

God calls us to have a counter-cultural view of love, sex, and dating. His plan for us is built around His love for us. How would you describe to your best friend that God's love for us is what drives His designs for love, sex, and dating?

display

These people who embraced their sinfulness so much that God turned them over to it, did not see it as worthwhile to acknowledge God (v. 28). List three worthwhile reasons to follow Jesus, and let His desires for your life lead your decisions.

Name two ways you can express how "worthwhile" it is to follow God's designs for love, sex, and dating on your social media platforms or in conversations with friends. Consider writing out what you want to post and creating an image to go along with your post!

> Pray that you would be a person who doesn't applaud evil, but always lives in and points others to the truth of who God is.

Relationship Goals

Section 4: HOW DO WE LOVE PEOPLE WHO DON'T FOLLOW GOD'S DESIGN?

day 25

STOP AND HELP!

discover

READ LUKE 10:25-37.

"Which of these three do you think proved to be a neighbor to the man who fell into the hands of the robbers?"
"The one who showed mercy to him," he said.
Then Jesus told him, "Go and do the same." — Luke 10:36-37

Most of the time when a girl becomes lost, one of three things happens. She might realize she is lost, stop, and get help. Or she might pretend she isn't lost and keep driving around, hoping to save face and figure out where she is. Or maybe she doesn't even realize she's lost and keeps going the wrong way.

If you are a Christian, you chose option one when you were lost in your sin. You realized you were lost and got the only assistance that could help—the sacrifice of Jesus on the cross. When it comes to admitting sin in their lives, most people fall into category two or three; they either try to fake it until they make it or they don't have any idea they are lost. We have to be willing to offer assistance to others when they need it—no matter what they believe—or we will never be able to help people caught in the second or third category.

For far too long, we have been like the priest and Levite in the parable of the Good Samaritan. We've looked at the broken world, seen the need, judged them as unclean, and crossed the street so we wouldn't get dirty, too. The aim of this devotion is not to shame you if this has been your attitude; it's to help you see how God can use you if you choose not to cross the street.

LifeWay Girls | Devotions

delight |

We don't have to agree with the ideas of girls who do not follow God's plan for love, sex, and dating to love and help them. The good Samaritan was good because he was compassionate. Name three ways you can be compassionate today.

display |

One of the best ways to be compassionate is to listen to those who are hurting. Next time a friend begins to talk about the pain in her life—even if it was caused by her own bad choices in relationships—choose to listen in love. Don't offer advice. Just listen. If she asks you what you think she should do, then you can offer biblical counsel based in gospel centric love.

Name one girl who you think might be hurting that you can reach out to today.

> Pray that you would learn how to be compassionate and love others without compromising the truth of the gospel. Then, pray that if the girl you named truly is hurting, you will get a chance to minister to her by listening.

day 26

SEEK AND SAVE

discover

READ LUKE 19:1-10.

"Today salvation has come to this house," Jesus told him, "because he too is a son of Abraham. For the Son of Man has come to seek and to save the lost."
— *Luke 19:9-10*

There's an old saying: "If you lie down with dogs, you'll get fleas." It means if you hang out with bad people, you'll be negatively influenced by them. We don't want our closest friends to be people who might lead us away from God. But we are called to be like Christ who came to seek and to save the lost (v. 10). Instead of being influenced by others, we should aim to influence others for Christ.

You probably know Zacchaeus best from the children's song, which points out that he was short. But his story is an example of Jesus doing something that the religious leaders of His time ridiculed Him for. They complained that He was associating with sinful people (v. 7). Just being welcomed by Jesus caused Zaccheaus to be influenced for good, offering to pay back anyone he had cheated in the past (v. 8).

The truth is, the sick need a doctor, and our world is full of sick people (Luke 5:31). How will they ever be healed if they don't see Jesus—the only Doctor who can help them? We know this Doctor because we have been healed by Him. We must help others come to Him to be healed as well. Therefore, we can't judge others as unworthy of His love because of their sinfulness. We must be willing to associate with "sinners" like Jesus was—not to be pulled into their sinfulness, but to reveal to them the only One who can heal their hearts.

LifeWay Girls | Devotions

delight |

Why did the religious leaders of Jesus' day look down on Him for spending time with people like Zaccheaus?

Look at Jesus' response to the religious leaders in verses 9 and 10. How can you respond to people who say we shouldn't associate with "sinners" at all?

What are two ways you can associate with people who don't know Christ without being drawn into some of the negative things they may do?

display |

Zacchaeus wanted to see Jesus, but he didn't seek Him out. Jesus made the first move toward a relationship with Zacchaeus. What is one thing you can do to make the first move toward someone who needs Jesus?

> **You probably know people who have very different views and practices about sex than what God desires. Take some time today to pray that you can be an influence on them, showing them the love of Jesus, who came to seek and save the lost.**

No temptation has come upon you except what is common to humanity. But God is faithful; he will not allow you to be tempted beyond what you are able, but with the temptation he will also provide the way out so that you may be able to bear it.

1 CORINTHIANS 10:13

day 27

TRUTH IN LOVE

discover

READ JOHN 4:1-26.

"I don't have a husband," she answered. "You have correctly said, 'I don't have a husband,'" Jesus said. "For you've had five husbands, and the man you now have is not your husband. What you have said is true." — John 4:17-18

Kids can be brutally honest, saying things most older people have learned not to say, like: "Your breath stinks!" or "Your food is gross!" or even "That dress makes you look fat!" Little kids aren't afraid to speak up about what they perceive to be true. Their honesty is accompanied by innocence, but there's also no doubting the love of a child, which often gives them a pass when they say these brutally honest things.

Jesus said some very blunt things to a woman He met in today's Scripture. But that wasn't the weirdest of the circumstances surrounding this story. For one, she was a woman, and it was seen as beneath a Jewish man to interact with women publicly (v. 27). She was also a Samaritan, and Jews did not associate with Samaritans at all (v. 9). And she came to get water in the heat of the day, most likely revealing that she wanted to avoid interaction with others by getting water when it was least convenient.[6]

Jesus called out her marriage record and that she was living with a person who was not her husband—which would have been offensive to most. Why didn't she slap Him and throw water in His face? Maybe because it wasn't what He said, but how He said it. Jesus word's weren't spoken in condemnation, but in love. It's possible to say difficult things to people when we say them in love.

Pray that God would grant you the ability to speak the truth in love.

delight |

Why do you think Jesus would risk His reputation to speak with this woman in Samaria?

Notice how the woman tried to change the subject when things got uncomfortable (v. 20). How can you stay on topic when people try to change the subject of Jesus' love for them?

In what ways, if any, can you identify with this woman? How is Jesus' response to her encouraging to you?

display |

You will encounter girls who are stuck in their sin. They will never listen to you if your tone is condescending or judgmental. If you want to love these girls well, seek to converse with them in a gentle and loving way—not avoiding the truth, but pointing toward God's goodness and mercy.

List three ways you can speak with love and gentleness toward others.

day 28

TOPPING THE CHARTS

discover

READ 1 TIMOTHY 1:5-11.

Now the goal of our instruction is love that comes from a pure heart, a good conscience, and a sincere faith. — 1 Timothy 1:5

The best songs usually top the Billboard charts, and we can't get them out of our heads. Their lyrics seem to be on replay long after the notes have ended on the radio. Some artists will stay at the top of the chart for weeks, but eventually someone else will release a song and take their place. No one would want to be on a list titled, "The Worst Songs of All Time." Yet, such a list exists. No one wants to top that chart!

As Christians, it has seemed for a while now that when it comes to sin, the item at the top of the list titled "Worst Sins of All Time" is sex. It seems that this type of sin sits on top of the sin charts and nothing can take its place at number one. At least, this is how people perceive sexual sin. Today's passage defines sexual sins as ungodly, but there were a lot of other things there, too (vv. 9-10). So why does sexual sin still top the charts as the worst sin?

It's possible people feel this way because the consequences of sexual sin are often quite drastic. Much pain and anguish results when people engage in sex outside of God's design. But worse consequences don't result in one sin being bigger in God's eyes than any other. Jesus went to the cross for the "white lie," murder, and everything in between.

All sin separates us from God. People who struggle with sexual sin aren't any worse than anyone else. They do not need or deserve a label that distinguishes them as a worse type of sinner than others. The bottom line is that they need instruction that will lead them to purity, a clear conscience, and sincere faith like everyone else.

delight |

The law pushes us away from wrong behavior (vv. 8-9). What causes heart change rather than just behavioral changes?

Paul mentioned sound teaching in verse 10. How can we know for sure that the teaching we are receiving is sound?

display |

The point of this devotion is not to minimize sin of any sort in any way. The desire is to help you see that there is no top-of-the-chart sin in God's eyes.

On a sticky note or index card, draw an equal sign on one side, and on the other, write out Romans 6:23. Put this in your Bible, marking that passage. Let it serve as a reminder that the end result of all sin is death, but the gift of God is life.

> Pray that God would make you aware of sin in your life, empower you to flee from it through the Holy Spirit, and turn you toward Jesus and His love.

day 29

REAL POWER

discover

READ 1 CORINTHIANS 2:1-5.

I came to you in weakness, in fear, and in much trembling. My speech and my preaching were not with persuasive words of wisdom but with a demonstration of the Spirit's power, so that your faith might not be based on human wisdom but on God's power. — 1 Corinthians 2:3-5

Television and movies don't resemble real life. We see this when a character gives a spontaneous speech to someone else and says exactly what the main character needs to hear. They never stumble over their words or say the wrong thing. They sound like they're rehearsing a speech that they've been working on for months—and it always perfectly makes the point.

Paul was incredibly honest about his speaking ability when he visited the Corinthians. He said he came in weakness, fear, and trembling (v. 3). That's hardly the picture-perfect presentation we see on television and in movies. But Paul was just the one who delivered the message. The Holy Spirit was the real source of power.

The power of the gospel is greater than your weakness to present it perfectly. The truth of the love of Christ overcomes any deficiency in your own ability. The power of the Holy Spirit can conquer any fear you might have. So, when it comes to speaking to someone about the truth of the gospel and God's design for love, sex, and dating, His power reigns above all. The best thing you can do is be humble and rely on the Holy Spirit to give you the right words to say. You don't have to be perfect; just be willing.

delight |

Describe a time when you tried to explain something to someone else and it didn't go as you had hoped.

How do we know that the power of the Holy Spirit is able to overcome any deficiency we may have in our own ability? (Hint: *Read Luke 12:12.*)

Why is it actually better that the Holy Spirit—and not your persuasive words—convicts someone's heart of what's true?

> **Pray that you will have opportunities to let the power of the Holy Spirit speak through you as you share His love with others.**

display |

Since we don't live in a movie or television show, one conversation probably won't convince anyone of the truth of God's Word. Instead, you'll have many conversations and build a relationship that grows and is sustained over time.

Name a girl you've talked with about the truth of God's Word. How did it go? What's one way you can keep the conversation going?

Name one girl you want to have a spiritual conversation with. What's one step you'll take toward doing that today?

day 30

CANCELING CANCEL CULTURE

discover

READ JOHN 8:2-11.

When Jesus stood up, he said to her, "Woman, where are they? Has no one condemned you?"
"No one, Lord," she answered. "Neither do I condemn you," said Jesus. "Go, and from now on do not sin anymore." —John 8:10-11

In our world today, there is a phrase used to describe when someone publicly fails or whose sins are exposed—usually of a sexual variety. It's called getting "canceled." It means these failures should erase this offender from public life and nullify her past—good and bad. By no means should abusers get a pass, and there should be consequences when laws have been broken and people have been hurt. But regardless of the sin committed, it's good news to know that God's grace remains for those who repent.

In today's Scripture, a group of Pharisees were trying to "trap" Jesus, and "cancel" a woman caught in adultery. They stood ready to cast judgment on her, and in doing so, they hoped to trap Jesus in a difficult place where He would have to either condone sin or allow a woman to be executed right in front of Him.

Jesus wasn't phased. The phrase He used to diffuse the situation is still very popular today: "The one without sin among you should be the first to throw a stone at her" (v. 7). This struck the Pharisees in the heart. They knew they weren't sinless, so they backed away one by one. All that was left was for Jesus to tell her that what she did was no big deal and to keep being herself, right? No. Jesus told

LifeWay Girls | Devotions

her He wasn't there to throw stones at her—or cancel her—but that she needed to change her ways. He didn't condone her sin; He just loved her toward the right path in life.

> **Thank God that He didn't cancel you. When you repented of your sins, He forgave you and loved you toward the right path for your life through His Son Jesus.**

delight |

Why do you think the older men walked away first (v. 9)?

Why do we often want to throw stones—harsh words, threats, and so on—at people who have fallen publicly?

How can we offer grace to people without condoning their sin?

display |

Name two ways you can follow Jesus' example not to condone sin, but to love and encourage people toward the right path in life.

There should be and are consequences for sin. This devotion is not meant to imply that people should be let off the hook for their actions. But where genuine repentance occurs, forgiveness and restoration should be made available as well. As Jesus' disciples, we should not be in the business of canceling people; we should live to and long to forgive and restore people when they've fallen. Because the truth of Romans 3:23 remains, we've all sinned and fallen short of the glory of God.

Tough Conversations About Sexuality

Chances are, whether you're talking about dating, sex before marriage, homosexual behaviors, or transgenderism, you'll find someone who vehemently disagrees—especially if you happen to follow a Christian sexual ethic. Jesus made clear in His Word that we would have trials, people would hate His followers because of Him, and that we would be different or "set apart" (Mark 13:13; John 15:19; 16:33). The pressures placed on Christians by the surrounding culture to conform to its ideals of sexuality and the increased division over issues of sexuality isn't a surprise to God. This is why He gives us His Word.

While the Bible doesn't outline something like "Six Steps to Having A Conversation with A Friend Who Doesn't Embrace the Biblical View of Sexuality," God's Word never fails to provide general principles that can guide us in interactions not explicitly stated in the Bible. Since this is the case, here's a general outline of biblical principles to help you have conversations with people who believe differently concerning sexual ethics.

Spiritually

Get to know God. We have access to God through Jesus, which is an amazing gift! But some of us still struggle with what it means to know God and how to develop a deeper relationship with Him. If we don't know God and His Word, then we won't know His design for sexuality. Thankfully, just as God provided a way for us to have a relationship with Him through Jesus, He also gave us His written Word to guide us to walk in His ways (2 Tim. 3:16-17). While that's pretty amazing already, God went a step further and sent the Holy Spirit to help us understand, remember, and live out what we learn from God's Word (John 14:26). As we get to know God, it will become clear just how much He loves all people—and that we are called to do the same (1 John 4:7-8).

Pray for compassion and understanding. Throughout Jesus' ministry, He consistently showed compassion. No matter how many miracles He worked, how the disciples and religious elite lacked understanding, or how many miles they walked, Jesus created space for people. He saw them—their flaws, their hopes, their needs, their hurts—and the Bible says, "he felt compassion for them, because they were distressed and dejected, like sheep without a shepherd" (Matt. 9:36). When we look around, it won't take long to see that people are still distressed and dejected, lost and confused. As Christians, we minister to people in the name of Jesus today, and He is our model for ministry (Matt. 9:37-38; 2 Cor. 20). As Paul said, we "put on the new self" when we become Christians, and part of that new self means we also "put on" the characteristics of "compassion, kindness, humility, gentleness, patience," and love (Col. 3:10,12-13).

Let the Holy Spirit lead. Only God is all-knowing, so it's important for us to understand that we won't know how to respond to everything. However, as we know, God sent the Holy Spirit to dwell within us, teaching us and helping us walk in His ways. In the Book of Luke, we're even told that the Holy Spirit will give us the right words at the exact moment we need them (12:12). Empowered by the Holy Spirit, we can live our lives characterized by "love, joy, peace, patience, kindness, goodness, faithfulness, gentleness, and self-control" (Gal. 5:22-23). Leaning into God's Word, our relationship with Jesus, and the Holy Spirit's leading are absolutely essential to having gospel-centered conversations—especially with those who believe differently.

Practically

Listen. This is more than just nodding every once in a while to acknowledge you're still physically present and not planning to interrupt. This means you really listen, even by paying attention to tone and body language. Think about what the person isn't saying. When they've finished speaking, summarize what they've said and check for understanding. For example, you might try something like: "What I hear you saying is _____. Is that correct?" If they say no and don't immediately launch into an explanation, try responding with "Okay, I would like to understand. Will you help me?"

Ask if you can share. Depending on how the conversation progresses, you may find that your friend would be open to hearing you. Once they've shared, you've checked for understanding, and they feel heard, then you might ask something like, "I appreciate your honesty and willingness to share with me. Would you mind if I share with you?" If they say no, be okay with that. Let it go, continuing to be compassionate and loving. If they say yes, be sure to express yourself with kindness, gentleness, and respect.

No one can predict what the outcome of a conversation will be—particularly when discussing a difficult topic upon which you disagree. However, your responsibility is to God, sharing His love, and walking in His truth. Never try to force your beliefs on someone—this will get you nowhere but stuck in reverse. Hold fast to God's truth, share it when He provides the opportunity, and love others no matter what.

Mixed Messages: Why Culture's Love is Different From God's Love

Is love really all we need, like the Beatles' song says? No, it isn't. Or at least, not love in the way it's so often portrayed in our music and movies today. Society's definition of love often veers toward self-serving, finding what's best for you, and fulfilling your happily-ever-after. God's definition of love, though, is almost the opposite. In God's design, our love—even romantic love—is designed to serve Him and present His image to the world.

What culture says isn't always right, even if it's popular. Or, at the very least, it doesn't tell the whole story. God's design for love is the most loving and the deepest love because He wrote the book on love. Literally, the Bible is His inspired Word, and it reveals His deep love for a broken and rebellious people throughout history. So, let's take a look at some common things culture tells us about love compared to what the Bible says about love.

Culture Says

Love is about physical attraction and connection.

Love is about satisfying your own desires.
You can stop loving someone when it's tough or your feelings change.

Marriage is disposable.

Love is what we see on social media.

Love means texting and snapchatting a lot.

Sex equals love.

I can love whoever I want, regardless of gender.

I have to become someone else or dress differently to be loved.

Love is an emotion.

LifeWay Girls | Devotions

God's Word Says

The most important foundation in marriage is a commitment to God and one another, a foundation of friendship and respect. Looks will fade over time, so we need to build relationships on what matters. (See Matt. 19:4-6, Eph. 5:33, and Heb. 13:4).

Love is about honoring God and others first. Love is not self-seeking. (See 1 Cor. 13:5.)

Marriage is a commitment to stick with your spouse on good days and bad, not just when you want to or when you're feeling the love. (See 1 Cor. 7:1-7,10-16.)

God hates divorce. Entering into marriage is a big deal because it is designed to be forever. (See Matt. 19:9.)

We should draw our pictures of love based on what we find in the Bible, not what we see on social media. Social media isn't always truthful, or at the very least, it's the very best moments of our lives. (See Eph. 5:31-32; 1 John 4:19.)

Love requires a deep and abiding knowledge of the other person. True love requires intimacy. (See Gen. 2:24.)

God's design is for us to be committed to God and to one another in marriage before we have sex. (See 1 Cor. 6:18-20; 7:2,8-9; and 1 Thess. 4:3-8.)

Marriage is between one man and one woman forever (Mark 10:6-9; Rom. 1:26-27).

We should love the way God designed us and live out of that. God defines us, not our relationship status. (See Gen. 1:28.)

Marriage models God's relationship with His people; it is a covenant (Isa. 54:5; Eph. 5).

Keep in mind that these biblical truths are based on the ideas of betrothal and marriage. Dating wasn't exactly a thing in Jesus' day. So, if you're dating someone who doesn't respect you, is unkind to you, speaks poorly about you, or just plain isn't following after Jesus—get out now. Someone who is truly seeking the Lord will not be perfect, but will honor, respect, and cherish you, putting your needs above their own.

Culture's version of love says we put ourselves first—finding what we want, then moving along if it changes. God's version of love may seem extreme to some of us, but it's designed to lead us into holiness, to draw us closer to Him, and to show the rest of the world what His love is like for those He calls His own. He gives us His name, He gives us His home, and He covers us always with His love.

Replay

Now that we've reached the end of our devotional, it might be difficult to remember the truths we've studied from the very beginning. So, let's take a minute to replay what we've learned so we'll be able to live according to God's design and share His truth about sex, dating, and relationships with others.

Section 1 (Days 1-9): God's Design for Sex
Come up with a book title and subtitle that summarizes God's design for sex. Write something that truly helps you more easily remember what you've studied in this section!

Title:

Subtitle:

Section 2 (Days 10-15): God's Design for Marriage and Gender
In Chasing Love, author Sean McDowell provides some helpful definitions related to gender and sexuality. Take a look at these and consider what you learned in section 2 of this devotional. Then, create a 30 second video summarizing all of the terms in your own words. Or you may choose to write out a short paragraph using each term, summarizing correctly what you've learned in this section.

- Transgender refers to a person who experiences incongruence between their biological sex and gender identity. Many transgender people describe their experience as feeling trapped in the wrong body.

- Gender dysphoria describes the psychological distress that some transgender people experience. While most people with gender dysphoria identify as transgender, some don't. And not all transgender people experience gender dysphoria. Transgender is an identity; gender dysphoria is a psychological condition.

- Intersex is a term for people who experience atypical development of their sexual anatomy and/or sexual chromosomes.

- Transgenderism is an ideology that aims to transform cultural understandings of sex and gender. The goal is to uproot the idea that humans are naturally sexed beings and to move society away from being shaped by the gender binary (or the way people are classified into two distinct groups as either male or female).[7]

Section 3 (Days 16-24): What is Outside of God's Design?

Draw a circle, and label the center with the words God's Design. Outside of the circle, write down anything you've studied that's outside of God's design. Consider writing out a 1-2 sentence "caption" for your image, describing what you've learned in this section.

Section 4 (Days 25-30): How Do We Love People Who Don't Follow God's Design?

Skim over these devotions once more and review the article "Tough Conversations About Sexuality." Then, think about someone you know who believes differently and isn't living God's design for sex and relationships—whether that's through sex outside of marriage, homosexual behaviors, or transgenderism. Ask God to show you how to love this person and speak to them with kindness. Pray that He would guide you to be understanding and compassionate—even though you disagree.

Now, imagine you've asked the person to share with you, and then ask, "May I share my heart with you, too?" Write out a letter using all the guidelines we've discussed and outline how you would gently and respectfully share about God's design with this person. Don't worry, you're not actually sending the letter—the point of this letter is to help you be prepared to respond in difficult conversations. When we're prepared, we're less likely to be caught off guard and respond in ungodly, unkind ways.

Safe Spaces

Talking about dating, sex, and relationships can be incredibly difficult, especially because it can mean embarrassment for the girl who has questions, struggles, or a story of abuse. Many girls don't come forward when they're seeking answers, struggling with sexual temptation or sin, or are being sexually abused. While it might feel embarrassing to talk about what's going on, opening up to someone who can help is the first step in healing.

Safe People You May Know

It's a good idea to identify now some safe people who have consistently created space for you, who will listen, who will remind you that you are loved, and who will help you. This might be a parent or guardian, close friend, family member, small group leader, teacher, student pastor, or pastor. **Who could you go to who would give you godly answers when you have questions about sex, are struggling with sexual temptation or sin, or are being sexually abused?**

Safe Places You Can Go

The reality is that sometimes someone you know and should be able to trust who is in a position of power is the one abusing you. If you do not feel safe with those who are close to you, reach out to an organization that can help. Here are some suggestions:

- Darkness to Light (D2l.org). Their website contains resources designated as national or by state (https://www.d2l.org/get-help/resources/). They can also be reached by calling 866.FOR.LIGHT

- RAINN (Rape, Abuse & Incest National Network). Call 800.656.HOPE to report sexual abuse or assualt. Or check them out online at https://www.rainn.org/ and choose the bright yellow "Live Chat" option at the top of the page to report abuse or assault.

- Lydia Discipleship Ministries (https://www.lydiadm.org/). This organization is founded to help people who are recovering from sexual abuse or any other kind of abuse, specifically abuse perpetuated by those in authority over them. They also provide resources for those who would like to help loved ones who are struggling. While they are not a reporting agency, you can contact them for help in recovery.

- Mercy Multiplied (https://mercymultiplied.com/). Based in Nashville, Mercy exists to help women break free from things like sexual abuse, depression, and addiction and also offers help to women with unplanned pregnancies. They offer a residential program as well as outpatient and online services.[8]

Safe Resources Concerning Sex and Dating

Books
Gay Girl, Good God by Jackie Hill Perry
Boundaries by Henry Cloud and John Townsend
Chasing Love (Teen Bible Study Book) by Sean McDowell
Love that Lasts by Jason and Alyssa Bethke
The Sacred Search by Gary Thomas
Love in Every Season by Debra Fileta
Passion and Purity by Elisabeth Elliot

Articles
"Three Pitfalls to Avoid When Dating" by Kevin DeYoung
(TGC, 2016)

"What does 'guard your heart' really mean in dating?" by Phillip Bethancourt
(The Ethics & Religious Liberty Commission [ERLC], 2015)

"16 quick takes on gender and sexuality" by Daryl Crouch
(ERLC, 2020)

"Is it harmful to date in high school?" by John Piper
(Desiring God, 2017)

Video
"Trillia Newbell's Word to Dating Couples" by The Gospel Coalition (TGC)
(TGC, 2018)

Quotes
"Dating with no regrets means keeping your focus on Jesus, so that no matter what happens in your relationships with others, your relationship with God remains intact."[9] —Debra Fileta

"Our sexuality is not our soul, marriage is not heaven, and singleness is not hell."[10] — Jackie Hill Perry

"Our culture encourages you to explore sexually as a way of finding and expressing who you are. God wants you to think about your sexuality in terms of whose you are."[11] —Juli Slattery

Sources

1. Matthew Henry, *The New Matthew Henry Commentary: the Classic Work with Updated Language*, ed. Martin H. Manser (Grand Rapids, MI: Zondervan, 2010), accessed via mywsb.com.
2. "O, Be Careful," Hymnary.org, accessed November 6, 2020, https://hymnary.org/text/o_be_careful_little_eyes_what_you_see?extended=true.
3. National Geographic Society, "Symbiosis: The Art of Living Together," April 17, 2019, https://www.nationalgeographic.org/article/symbiosis-art-living-together/.
4. "Grand Canyon Mule Rides," GrandCanyon.com, January 24, 2019, https://grandcanyon.com/planning/grand-canyon-mule-rides/.
5. "6 Ways Pilots Get Confused In The Clouds, And How To Prevent It," Online Flight Training Courses and CFI Tools, accessed November 10, 2020, https://www.boldmethod.com/learn-to-fly/aeromedical-factors/spatial-disorientation-vestibular-illusions-and-how-to-prevent-each-one-of-them/.
6. The Glory Is Revealed Among the Despised: A Samaritan Woman (4:1-42) - The IVP New Testament Commentary Series - Bible Gateway, accessed November 11, 2020, https://www.biblegateway.com/resources/ivp-nt/Glory-Is-Revealed-Among-Despised.
7. Sean McDowell , *Chasing Love*, Teen Bible Study (Nashville, TN: LifeWay Christian Resources, 2020).
8. "Resources: Sexual Abuse," Focus on the Family, November 3, 2020, https://www.focusonthefamily.com/resources-sexual-abuse/.
9. Fileta, Debra K. True Love Dates: Your Indispensable Guide to Finding the Love of Your Life. Zondervan, 2018.
10. Perry, Jackie Hill. Gay Girl, Good God: The Story of Who I Was and Who God Has Always Been. B&H Publishing Group, 2018.
11. Slattery, Julianna. Sex and the Single Girl. Moody Publishers, 2017.